Stories from Pangnirtung

Stories from Pangnirtung

Illustrated by Germaine Arnaktauyok

Foreword by Stuart Hodgson

Hurtig Publishers / Edmonton

Hurtig Publishers
10560 105 Street
Edmonton, Alberta

ISBN 0-88830-109-X

Contents

Foreword

Stuart Hodgson
Commissioner of the
Northwest Territories

Early European visitors have written of their encounters with the Arctic and its people. Anthropologists have provided many volumes about Inuit customs and lifestyles. Novelists have interpreted and stylized the North. Journalists have recently discovered its news value.

But to know of the past, to understand the present, and to contemplate the future, the more rewarding source of information about the Arctic remains the Inuit people themselves.

These stories from Pangnirtung offer the opportunity of listening to northern people as they speak from the heart. Their words, translated from the Inuktitut language, express knowledge, emotion, and history.

By reading these stories and recollections, one may appreciate the struggles of life, the good times and bad times of a people in transition.

Through these pages, the people of Pangnirtung share their memories, their values, and their aspirations. Their words convey the importance of the whale and caribou, the difficulty of mastering a harsh environment, the joy of life and the prominence of death, the fears and hopes of tomorrow.

By recognizing and recording the thoughts of our northern elders, these stories from Pangnirtung will strengthen an awareness and respect of the Inuit heritage and culture by younger and future generations.

Pangnirtung has a particularly interesting history. Before the present community developed as a geographic identity in the 1920s, the Inuit people of this region of Baffin Island lived in scattered camps along

Cumberland Sound. Although the Sound was "discovered" by the English captain John Davis in 1585, almost no contact was made with the "whiteman" until three hundred years later when the area was used as a base camp for a group of German scientists participating in the International Polar Year of 1883.

Towards the turn of the century, the whaling market attracted visitors for a dozen years or so, but it was the opening, from 1921 to 1926, of a Hudson's Bay Company trading post, a police detachment, and small school and hospital which first put the community on the whiteman's map.

Now with the establishment of Canada's first Arctic national park just north of the community, the Pangnirtung Fiord will likely become the path by which many people from around the world come to view the magnificent mountains, glaciers, valleys, and waters of the Cumberland Peninsula.

As the national park will preserve the natural environment and beauty of the Pangnirtung region, so will this book help to preserve the history of its people.

To the people of Pangnirtung, I offer my congratulations and thanks for the initiative and effort which has resulted in this collection.

To the reader, I suggest you listen carefully to the true experts of the North.

January 1976 |

We used to live like that in those days

Told by
Jamasie Alivatuk
aged 67
of Pangnirtung

I remember very little of when I was a small boy. I do remember the days when my father used to take me with him whenever he went out seal hunting. I had no mother. My mother died when I was very small. My father tried hard to be both the mother and father to me. When there were baby seals to hunt, my father took me with him because I had no one else to take care of me. Whenever he had caught one, he used to let me put a hook through it and I'd think I had caught it myself. There were a lot of baby seals those days. Sometimes our *kamootiks* would be filled with them.

When night came, my father would make us an igloo on the sea ice. While my father made an igloo, I'd fall asleep on the *kamootik* and didn't wake up even when he carried me inside. I couldn't help him with anything because I was still too young to help. He would wake me up after he had cooked seal meat. I would wake up to a warm igloo and some meat waiting for me to eat. After I had eaten all I could, I would fall asleep again.

I remember, too, that while my father and I were out hunting I was always getting cold hands. My father made me mitts of baby sealskin or rabbit skin. They were very uncomfortable. I couldn't take hold of anything, but they were better than nothing. My father did not quite know how to sew because he is not a woman to do the women's work. He did his best to clothe me.

In the summertime we used to go out to Nutseelik by a small boat. This was years ago when I was still a small boy. I don't quite recall what year it was. We went caribou hunting up to Nutseelik. When we landed, we used to go back and forth to the boat, unloading the things in it. I didn't do anything to help because I was still too young, but it was always a lot of fun watching the others work.

When we went up to Nutseelik, it sometimes took us about three to four days. We would stop for the night on the trip. Sometimes we had to walk to where we were camping for the night. When we reached the lake, it seemed that we were on the sea; the lake was very big. In the mornings, all we heard were bird sounds and it was always nice to hear them. The only people we saw there were the people we were with and that's not so many. The lake is always like that in summer and I guess it is still like that right now. I haven't been there for many years now, so I don't quite know how it is. I sometimes think about the place even though I might not ever go there again.

We would go by a small boat to where we were heading. We didn't have any motors those days. All we used were paddles and sails. We would pass islands on the way and we would stop on these islands and hunt caribou because there used to be so many on the islands.

Whenever we moved to a new camp we had to carry most of our things with us. We had to take the spears, harpoons, hooks, and some skins to make our *kamiks* and clothes. When you put together the people and their belongings in a small boat, the boat becomes quite full; so we tried our best to carry as much of our belongings as we could.

Everyone had to help carry the things we would be needing. The dogs, and the women and men carried things on their backs. The small children who couldn't carry or help with anything just walked along and when they got tired or sleepy the fathers would carry them on their backs along with the rest of the things that they were carrying.

The dogs would carry our food on their backs. They carried seal meat, fish, caribou meat, or anything that we lived on. We only brought Eskimo food, not the white man's food. In those days we did not have tea or biscuits but just plain meat, raw or cooked; so we never brought along the white man's food, even if their food is good. The only things that were white man's that we brought along with us were the bullets for our guns because it was a lot easier to hunt seals or other animals with a gun; so we brought bullets along.

When we had reached the place where we would camp for the summer and we had everything unloaded, we would then go up in the hills and hunt. Sometimes the men would just go for a walk where there might be caribou, and when they saw a herd they would go after them. When they had enough caribou to carry they would go back to their tents where their wives were waiting.

When I grew up, before I had a wife, I'd go out for caribou with the others. We could have caught a lot of caribou if we tried but we didn't because we had to think about carrying them, and we also had to think about our small boats which do not carry too much. But if we had caught

too many we would store some so it wouldn't go bad while we were gone. That's the time when caribou had much fat in their bodies. Sometimes it seemed there were too many caribou skins to carry back, but they were the only things we made our clothes out of; so we had to bring them along with us. Before we carried them we would roll them up to their smallest size and then carry them on our backs along with the meat.

When we returned to our camps we would then unload the meat. We didn't just unload the meat and leave everything here and there; we had to put the meat into sealskin bags which we made. Sometimes we would use the sealskins which were the old *kayak's* cover. They were very good because they kept the meat fresh and dry. Even if we put them in water, the water wouldn't get into them. The sealskins were the best to make bags out of.

For clothes we had sealskins and caribou skins. We had no other things to wear. They were always warm. We had to hunt for our clothes, too, for the winter that was coming was going to be very cold. Nowadays the people no longer hunt for clothes because they buy them from the Hudson's Bay Company stores.

We used to live like that in those days. We played games, too. Not with the things that the young people today use. Now they ride around in ski-doos. We played games like kicking a ball. We'd play a lot of games. We always played in the evenings just like the young people do these days. Now they have things like ski-doos to play with and ride. I don't think very many young people nowadays know how to do things like we did in the old days. All they know now is the white people's ways. They don't quite know how to live like a real Eskimo.

I still haven't forgotten how to make a *kayak*. The *kayaks* in those days were used a lot but now the people no longer use them. We no longer think even to make them. *Kayaks* were very useful in those days. If you hadn't had a *kayak* when you were out at the floe edge you'd lose the seal you had caught. We carried seal meat inside the *kayak* because that was the only way we could bring home some meat for our wives and children to eat.

My wife was good at making *kayaks*. She knows how to sew and how to make threads to sew with; so it was quite easy to make things out of skins with the help of my wife. I had two *kayaks* all the time, one for the use in the summer and the other for winter. The winter *kayak* had to fit on the *kamootiks* so that whenever we wanted to go out to the floe edge it would be easy to handle. The winter *kayak* was made out of about eight large skins.

We hunted in cold or warm weather because that was the only way we could feed our families and friends. Nowadays we don't hunt because we can buy food from the stores and we can buy our clothes from the stores, too, but in those days we had to go hunting almost every day for food and clothing. Sometimes it was hard to get food and clothing, but we all tried very hard to get some.

We depended on everything we had. We depended on our dogs, boats, *kayaks*, or anything we owned those days, but now the people don't really need these things to hunt with because there is a Hudson's Bay Store where they can buy their food and clothing. In the old days it was a hard life we were leading.

We had to make our winter tents which we would live in until the snow was just right to make our winter houses out of snow. It sometimes took about three days to make our tents out of sealskins or mustache sealskins. In those days wood was hard to get so we only used skins to make our tents. We'd make two tents, one a little smaller than the other. Our women gathered weeds or plants to make the beds or to put between the outer and the inner walls of the tents.

The best things to carry things with were the mustache sealskins which were the skins from which we made our *kayaks* or boats. They were very good to put some little things in that might get wet, because the skins were waterproof.

Before white men came to Pangnirtung, we moved here for there were more fish to catch; we didn't know that we were going to live here for always. We never even thought there were going to be people living in Pangnirtung. There are now so many here. There used to be a lot of caribou around here in the old days. Now there seem to be none at all.

We used to walk sometimes in cold days when it was raining or windy. We didn't care how the weather was as long as we got to the places where we planned to camp for the summer. Sometimes it was fun walking in different weathers, sometimes I got pretty mad, but I couldn't do anything about it; so it was best to forget about being mad at the weather.

When I was old enough to know how to take care of myself, and when I had gotten a wife, but before I had children, my father gave me a team of dogs so that I could go out for food to feed my wife and myself. I got my first team of dogs at the age of seventeen. Ever since the time I got my first dogs, I've had dogs of my own. Even now I have a few dogs and I am now sixty-five years old.

With the dogs I could go anywhere I wished to go. We depended on them in those days. If we didn't have dogs we couldn't go anywhere far; so we depended on the dogs we had. I'd go out for food to feed my family and others. It was a hard life but it was fun. I'd go out on the ice for seals or on land for caribou or small animals.

In those days a man would let others in the same camp know that he would be going out on the ice or anywhere so that the others would know where to look for him in case he didn't return on the day he said he'd return.

The life now is so different from the life we were leading in those days. We were living in different camps with very few people in the camp. Right now almost all the people who used to live in small camps near Pangnirtung have moved to one place. Everything seems to be so different now. The people seem to have changed, too. Some of them don't seem to share the things they have caught with others, while in the early days we shared every little thing we caught with other people. Life has changed very much now.

We were always kept busy all year around, getting food or skins for our clothes or tents or anything that we made out of skins.

I was born in the spring, in a camp called Oomanayoak, or Blacklin Island.

I remember when I was a small boy in Oomanayoak, our parents taught us how to hunt by letting us hunt small animals like ptarmigan and rabbits. I was the only child in my family. My father taught me everything he knew about hunting. He died when I was still a little boy, but I tried to follow everything he taught me, and when I went seal hunting I sometimes didn't get what I was after because I was too young.

My father was a whaler. We owned a house which the Americans gave to him. My father was the leader of the people down at Oomanayoak. When the Americans no longer came to Oomanayoak, the only white men that came then were the English and the Scottish whalers. They wanted my father to trade the house to them, and they got what they wanted. They got the house for a boat, rifle, and some boxes of pilot biscuits. We had never seen any white men's food and things. We never did see sugar before; the only sweet thing we had tasted was jam.

We kids made small *kamootiks* out of whale bones so we could go sliding from hills, just like the kids do nowadays. For ropes we used sealskins. We would tie the rope to the *kamootiks* and pull them.

While we were growing up our fathers used to teach us how to make igloos out of snow. One has to have the right kind of snow to build one. For the first time we would make a small one, and as years went by we would be much better than we had been. That is how we learned. When we went hunting later we could make our own igloos without any help.

How we hunted whales

Told by
Markosie Pitsualak
aged 81
from Pangnirtung

18

From Oomanayoak we would go to a place where there were animals to hunt. In those days we didn't have to follow any law set down about hunting, but instead we, the Eskimos, had a meeting about where there were animals to be caught; the men had their own meetings about hunting. Now we have to follow the hunting laws, like the ones that say a person can catch so many animals per year.

The men would gather and tell each other where they would be in the winter if they were going to leave Oomanayoak. In winter the people who had dog teams would leave for a better place to hunt, but the families who didn't have dogs stayed where they were, and sometimes in the winter they would go hungry because they had to go on foot to hunt. But most of the time the snow was too soft to walk on. It was always hard on the men who didn't have dogs, but to the men who had dogs, it was easy.

When I grew up, I got married in Oomanayoak, and later on I went after whales with the English and Scottish whalers. My wife and I had two children and moved out of Oomanayoak to another camp, and we lived there for forty-five years. I was getting old by then.

The only boats we used in those days were *kayaks*. We used to make our boats from sealskins and mustache sealskins. If we used sealskins we used about twenty-four skins, and if we used mustache sealskins we would only use five or six. For sails we used the long intestines of the mustache seals. We cut them up and sewed them together. In those days we didn't have fabric to make things with, but we always had skins.

We went out in *kayaks* for seals. Whenever one got a seal, the *kayaks* were rowed together, and out there in the water, we'd haul the seal on top of the *kayak* and skin it and cut up the meat. Then we'd rinse the meat in the water and split it between us all. Not one bit of seal was wasted. Even the blood of the seal was not wasted. We put the blood inside the skin. We did the same with the mustache seals.

It was very nice to see all the *kayaks* come in from hunting. When the men reached land the men cooked the seal meat for everyone to eat. They would call all the people to eat. The old and young would be separated. The old people were slow eaters. Whenever we gathered together to eat with them, it seemed to me that there was not very much left for them because they ate very slowly. We played games when we were together, like telling stories by song, using a drum. The younger people took part in it, too. Everyone always had something to eat.

We always helped the older people and tried to be kind. Before my father died, he used to tell me to be kind to older folk and to bring water for those old people who did not have families to help them. I used to bring them water and salt from the bay, and they'd be very thankful, and they would say that because I was kind to them I would live to be an old man. I believe them because I am now old. I still remember those days. They don't bring food to old people now.

We went whaling in May one year; it was very cold. We were camped at the water's edge. There were a lot of white whales that year, but we were after sperm whales; so we were not allowed to shoot at the white whales. While we waited for a whale, we would go seal hunting on the ice, but we had to keep watch for our leader's signal that he had sighted a sperm whale. We had to leave the seals we had caught and run to the boat, or we would be left behind. Once, because I didn't want to leave a seal behind, I hurried towards the boat, pulling the seal right behind me, but when they got the boat out into the water, I had to leave the seal and run for the boat. I barely made it that time.

We hadn't seen a sperm whale for awhile. Then one came up from under the ice and was just floating around because he didn't see us. Four boats went after it. The boats were very fast even though the men only paddled. The first boat to reach the whale shot it while the others stopped to wait. The men threw spears at the whale and it went down into the sea. We timed it to see how long the whale was underwater. Sometimes they went underwater for three hours. When the whale went underwater, the front of the boat dipped very low, almost submerged. He headed towards the ice and we thought that the boat was going to break in pieces, but, when we slid onto the ice, there was nothing broken.

One of the men jumped out of the boat while we were on the ice because he was so afraid we would all die. Our leader shouted not to get off. When we started going again, we left the man that got off there because he didn't have time to get back on the boat.

When the whale surfaced the men shot it again and threw spears at it.

The spears were tied to rope on the boat. The whale went around and around, and the boat went right behind it. Later, when the whale died, we pulled it towards the ice. We let it float in the water and then we went to sleep.

The next morning our leader told us that we would not sleep again until we had reached Oomanayoak. We could see the land was very far from where we were and knew that it was going to take long and hard work. Our leader had told us we were not going to sleep until we reached land. So, we stayed up, working for three and a half days and three and a half nights without sleep, because the leader didn't want to lose the whale.

The leaders never seemed to get sleepy at all. We paddled slowly, pulling the big sperm whale right behind us, and it was very hard work. Sometimes when we rowed we fell asleep, and if our leader found us asleep, he banged a stick on our paddles and right away we would be wide awake...for a little while.

The land seemed so far away. Oomanayoak was very far from where we were. There was never any wind when we were pulling the sperm whale. We always wished for some, but, even if we'd had any, it wouldn't have helped because the sperm whale was far too heavy, even for the wind. When we finally reached the land, we were so tired we only took our blankets out and went to sleep without doing anything else.

There were always men waiting for us on land. When they saw that we pulled a whale behind us, they were so happy that they fired guns into

the air and came over to help pull it in. As soon as we landed the whale, we started to work on it. The women helped with the work. They were happy because it was fun. We skinned it and took the fat off; we pulled the blubber further inland. We had to wear special boots when we worked on the whale and needed a ladder to climb on top of it. After we finished the body, we went to work on the head.

We had to get the pouches where the whales stored their food because the whalers wanted them, too. Two men could walk inside the whale's mouth and work because the sperm whale is such a large animal. It took two days just to get the tongue out because when the tide came in we had to stop. We cleaned the pouches and put them in bags and put the blubber in barrels. After we had done all this work, we had to clean and wash the insides of the boats for next year when we went out again to go whaling.

In the fall, when the ship came in, the Eskimos went to work again. It took two men to carry one bag of the whale pouches. After the pouches were put on the ship, the barrels were loaded. In the barrels there were seal blubber, mustache seal blubber, and other kinds of blubber.

When the ship left, a horn was blown at a house, and we would go to the person who had blown the horn. We were going to get something for working. We never got what we wanted. We didn't get any money even though we worked so hard on the whales. We got what the whalers gave us. The person who had shot the whale would get a boat and a rifle. We, the whalers, didn't get what we deserved to get. Now that I think about it, we were all fooled. For working so hard we got a new pair of pants, shirt, smoking pipe, and tobacco. The pipes we got were, I guess, made out of clay or stone. I don't see them around these days. Our wives who helped cut up the blubber and put it into barrels got things, too. Putting blubber into barrels and cutting it up was hard work. They would get things like pots, kettles, material, tobacco, smoking pipes, and soap.

Then the white whaler chose his men to go out on the next whale hunt with him. When they asked me to go with them, I was so happy to go. They had to let you know a few months ahead before they went out whaling. Even if it was hard work, I really wanted to go, and when I was chosen to go I was so happy.

I started remembering when I was a small boy. I was born in a camp called Oomanayoak, English name, Blacklin Island. I kind of remember the lake that we walked alongside. I see it sometimes, and sometimes I don't see it at all.

I remember seeing two men working on a caribou, but I didn't know what they were doing. Later on I found out they were skinning the animal. My mother told me that there were a lot of caribou on the lake when I was born. I kind of remember it, but I seem to have been dreaming.

I remember whenever I started crying my mother used to pat me on the back. I remember being baptised by a minister, along with two girls who were born the same time I was born. After the service we went home to our tent, and when we got there the tent seemed to be small inside.

When I turned a year old we left Oomanayoak by dog team for a camp which is called Seegaeyah, where there were no white people. My mother carried me there in her *amoutik*. Whenever I started crying my mother would get me out of her *amoutik*. It was always very cold. She would wrap me with the front part of her *amoutik* and try to warm me with her hand by rubbing my skin.

We reached a camp called Nutinae, which is a few miles from Seegaeyah. There was an old house there. My mother and I went inside it and found it was pretty warm. Inside the house my parents and others ate meat while the children and I ran around the place playing games. I didn't watch what I was doing when suddenly I cut myself with a knife. I hadn't listened to my mother when she told me not to run around too much or else I would get hurt; I had cut myself and it was my own fault.

The next day we started out again and when evening came I saw lights in front of us and realized we had reached a camp. The camp was Seegaeyah. At the camp I turned four years old.

There was a boy I used to play with at Seegaeyah. His name was Koagak. When Koagak and I became older we used to hunt rabbits or ptarmigan. On the hunting trips Koagak had a rifle, and he used to smoke. Once while we were resting, I asked my friend to give me his cigarette, rifle and some bullets, and right away, he gave them to me. Then I told him that I was going to use his cigarette as a target. He said his father told him never to waste bullets on something that is not an animal, but I told him that his father would only think that we were shooting at animals when he heard the shots; so we started to shoot at my friend's cigarette. Even when we were sure we hit it, it was still there. Now, I had a shotgun with me. I told Koagak to watch his poor cigarette while I shot it, but when I hit it we didn't know where it went.

One spring a bunch of us kids went out walking in the evening. While we walked I suggested that we should try to catch some birds for pets; so we all started to run after birds. Koagak tripped and fell. I finally caught one and kept it for my pet. Then I realized we were on the frozen lake, and I remembered my father telling me not to go on the ice when he wasn't with me. We started to head back home, but before we reached the edge of the land, I heard a crack. The ice had split, and I was in water. The other kids helped me out. I hadn't realized I was squeezing the bird so hard, but when I looked to see if it was still alive, it was dead.

We used to play a lot of games at night as our parents slept. I remember once when we played house, I was the father, and I'd go out to hunt. It was dark so I didn't know where I was stepping, and I went into a mudhole and got mud all over myself; so I had to go home and go to bed.

When summer came my father was asked to work for a white man, getting some blubber to make oil. We left camp and camped somewhere else so my father could hunt better. Once, while my father was out hunting, my mother and I saw geese land beside our house behind the hills. She wanted to shoot at them but, because I was the oldest child in the family and had never shot a goose, I asked my mother to give me the gun so I could shoot the geese. She gave the gun to me and I left. When I reached the geese they flew away; so I made geese sounds and when they flew over my head I shot at them and got the leader. I went home and we had goose for supper. The next day we headed back to our camp because we had enough blubber for the white man.

After we had reached our main camp that summer, I started working for the white man, going out whale hunting to make a little money. When I got paid, I'd buy food, material, and tobacco for my parents, even though I didn't smoke.

In the same summer, a friend of mine, Joanasie, and I went rabbit hunting. I caught two rabbits; so I gave my gun to him so he could get his own rabbits. But when he started to shoot, he wasn't shooting in the right direction. I took the rifle back from him and told him he shouldn't be using a rifle because he was just going to waste the bullets on nothing. We started to head back to our camp. As we were walking, my friend said he heard something from behind; so we started running. We only had one gun. I decided that I should shoot in the direction in which he pointed, and after I shot we heard something. We then found out that the thing we were hearing was the spring in my rifle. It was loose, and that was the thing that my friend heard. That was the time I was pretty dumb for my age.

When fall came we were all hungry for food. We had seen a walrus out in the bay, not too far from land. We shot it but it was a very thin walrus. We didn't like it even though we were hungry.

A cousin and I went out in our rowboat to hunt some birds. We had caught a few birds when we heard shots, and when we learned what the people were shooting at, we joined them. They were after white whales. There were lots of whales in the fiord. The men caught, maybe, twenty whales, and that is the most I've ever seen caught. There were such a lot of whales that the men were throwing spears at them. I was using a rifle and shooting them, but I was shooting at the wrong places of the whale's body. One had to shoot at the neck part, but at that time I was not a very smart boy. I was just learning to become a man.

Then we left Seegaeyah for a better place to hunt, but even in the new camp we were going hungry. There was no food to be found anywhere. We had a leader, but we were all going hungry. I remember a girl who had no husband or father to hunt food for her and her mother. The girl used to go to other houses in her mother's *kamiks*. I really felt sorry for her, but I couldn't help her at all. When she came to our place, I asked her what she would like to have, and she said she would like to have the fox tail, so I gave it to her. I cried very much because I gave her something to eat that is not really something to eat. I hated myself for it.

Once when the girl and her mother were alone in their house, there came a polar bear. The women didn't have any gun or spears to fight the bear, so they stayed inside. The bear climbed on top of their house and slid down. After a while the bear left.

I remember the girl was always kind to people. She used to ask us to come over to her house to tell us about the love of the Lord Jesus. She and her mother died from starvation that winter.

After a while we moved back to our old camp, Seegaeyah, because we were going hungry in the new camp. My father and his brother-in-law went back and forth with only three dogs to bring all the people back to Seegaeyah. There were some children who lost their parents when the parents died from starvation. These children were living with us. Their father had been badly frozen, and he had soon died. There were no doctors in those days to take care of us when we were sick. The people died because there was no medicine or doctors to help the Eskimos.

We left Seegaeyah on the boat the following summer to a place where there was a white man who wanted to help the Eskimos. He and his family were there, and the name that the people gave him was Meetimak. He had a trading post and got supplies through the ships that came every summer with supplies for the trading post. The trading post sold guns, ammunition, and other supplies.

Then we moved to Meegnutok because the Eskimo leaders said it was a better place to live. But, when we were there, we went hungry again, and this time it was worse than the first time. I lost a brother and a sister when they starved to death. After this place we moved back to Seegaeyah, and there we lost our parents. One died from a disease which was in the arm, and the other died because something was wrong with the throat. When they died my younger brothers and sisters went to live with my uncle and his family, but they also died; so I went to my grandfather and, when he died, I went to live with Nueeyaot. Sometimes I lived with Adla. Mostly I was living with Adla. He was the one in his family who kept me alive by feeding me. He'd give me his old clothes to wear.

When I was twelve years old I went caribou hunting with the rest. We were all walking. While I was trying to cross the river, one *kamik* came off and went down and we couldn't get it; so the men told me to go back to the camp. I headed back because I only had one *kamik* on my feet. But I used the caribou parka that I got from Adla to make myself another one and returned to the others, but they weren't waiting for me. Then I crossed the river and I got my *kamiks* very wet. I took them off and went barefoot carrying them. My feet started to hurt so that I could hardly walk. I squeezed the water out of the *kamiks* and put them on.

A little while later, I found three caribou. I had only three bullets. I made sounds like a caribou and soon they came towards me. I took a shot but didn't hit one. The biggest caribou was so near that I could see the eyes, the nose. I took two more shots but didn't hit them. They were going away so I stood up and made myself look like a caribou, and the biggest caribou came back. He was getting so close that I was getting scared, and I ran away from it. Then the men found me. They went after the three caribou and caught all three of them. We headed back to our camp carrying the caribou on our backs.

My wife and I were born at Blacklin Island when whalers began coming to that place. I started to remember when white men came. I remember one man the Eskimos called Ookamak. His real name was Mr. Page. There were others like Ilatak and Ilatakao but I don't remember their English names. In those days there were quite a few white men coming up North for sperm whales. Men came from England, Ireland, Scotland, and from other parts of the world. I think they came from all over the world to hunt sperm whales here in the North. They had Eskimos to help them with the whaling. Everyone worked hard when a whale was caught.

The white men were not all whalers. There were missionaries, traders, and others. The whalers were after the fat of the sperm whales. They'd send the fat by the ships that came up here every summer. They also took skins, with or without blubber on them, but mostly with the fat on.

The Eskimo name of the leader of the whalers was Anulik. He was getting pretty old then and I have heard that he no longer lives. He had spent almost ten years of his life with the Eskimos by the time World War I was on. He ran out of his kind of food. The Eskimos kept him alive by feeding him fish, geese eggs, and some caribou meat. He said that he liked those best to eat. In winter he would go out with the Eskimo men to hunt for his food. Every year he was taught by the Eskimos how to keep alive, until it was safe again to go back to his homeland.

When he left the North for his homeland, he had forgotten how to speak English. He had three children who were all grown up when he

*The things that
the eskimos did*

Told by
Jim Kilabuk
aged 74 from
Blacklin Island

34

went back to them. When they sat down to eat supper, the father didn't know how to speak any English so he spoke Eskimo and didn't realize it at all. His children, when they heard him speak, thought he was out of his mind. Anulik only spoke Eskimo because that was the only language the people of the North spoke. I guess his children didn't know that the things their father spoke were words that meant something.

Years later there were only Eskimo leaders to lead the people. Before, they used to have white men to lead them but now they had Eskimo leaders even though there were still white men coming by ship.

But sometimes we were afraid of the white man because he was so different from all of us. We loved the white man's food, but we were always afraid of him. When we passed their windows we would sometimes crawl on the snow so the white man wouldn't see us passing his house. We liked their food best but we were afraid of them. We were very silly and dumb in those days when we were kids.

I used to think, too, whenever I'd look at the tall mountains when I was small, I always thought that the mountains were touching the sky and that if I went on top of the mountains I could touch the sky when I reached up. We were sure dumb in those days.

When we wanted to play outside and slide down the hills, we didn't have small *kamootiks* to slide with. We were poor and there wasn't any wood to make our small *kamootiks;* so we'd use ice. We'd shape the ice to

look like a *kamootik* and make a hole in the front so that we could put a

rope through it. After making our *kamootik*, we would then climb up to the top of the hill and slide down and when we reached the place where there was no snow, our *kamootik* would break because they were made out of ice.

We always had fun sliding down the hills, but we had to make another *kamootik* when we reached the bottom because they always broke. It was hard making our *kamootiks*, but if we wanted to slide down the hills we had to make them first so that we'd have something to slide with. We had skins to slide down the hills with sometimes, but our mothers made clothes and had other uses for them; so we didn't always have skins to play with. Sometimes we tried to slide down with just our clothes but it wasn't much fun.

We used to make our own gum to chew in the spring. When spring came and the sun came out, our fathers, or even we, made gum out of old feathers or the hair of the sealskins, and added to it caribou muscles so that it would stretch when chewed, just like any gum nowadays. When we made them, they never tasted the same; some tasted better than the others. Sometimes we would add some cooked blood so that the gum would turn brown and have a better taste to it. They weren't as sweet as the bubble gums are today but they were good.

We also used to play games with the seal flipper bones after they were cooked. Each bone had its own name. We had lots of fun playing with the bones. Everyone used to play with them, even the old people.

With some games we learned while playing. We learned different things while playing the bones. We learned how to spear or harpoon a seal or other animals. We sometimes put holes in a piece of sealskin and tied it to a string and hung it up so that we could try to put a stick through the holes. That was to teach us that some animals were harder to catch than others. So we learned how to spear before we were old enough to hunt.

In those days we were hungry. Sometimes the animals that we ate were hard to catch, and when there was no more food to eat, we had to eat sealskins. We pulled the fur off the skins and burned it so that we could eat the skins. They tasted awful but there was nothing else to eat. We also ate some fat. We cooked it in a pot and ate it just like that because there was nothing else. When we were hungry we would eat anything that was not poison or bad to eat. We ate anything to keep alive.

In those days we were all poor. Even the white men were poor. To keep warm they had old cans to use for stoves and wood to keep their fires going, and the Eskimos had *kooliks*, stoves made out of soapstones, to keep the igloos warm. If the *koolik* went off at night the whole of the inside of the igloo became very cold. The first person who got up in the morning would make the fire to try to make the igloo warm again. It took a long time to warm up but we didn't have any other thing to warm up the whole igloo. When we were only going to be out hunting for a day or two, we didn't bring blankets with us. We slept with our parkas on, but if we were going to be out for a week or longer we would bring blankets.

When the *koolik* was on, one man would melt snow or ice for us to drink, and after we all had had some water to drink, he would then cook seal meat so that we'd have something to eat. One man had to stay up all night to watch that the *koolik* didn't go off so that we could have something to eat when we got up in the morning.

After we all had eaten, we would then go out and hunt for food to take back to our camp. When I was old enough, I went out hunting with the men. We had to wait beside a seal hole for a seal to come up, and we would often wait a long time. We sometimes waited all day and all night without eating or drinking. When my father went out to wait for a seal to come up from the seal hole, he would bring along his Bible to keep him company. He would read while waiting for a seal. I think most of the older folks brought something to read.

There was one guy I remember well because I used to go out hunting with him. He was half blind because he was old. His name was Ootookiak. Whenever he saw a seal near he would crawl over to it on his hands and knees. When he thought the seal was near enough to shoot he would get his shotgun and shoot the seal. But, when he went to run to it, it always seemed that he took only two or three steps and the seal was at his feet.

There was one time when he was going after what he thought was a seal. He found he couldn't reach near enough to the seal. He was going after it a long time, but couldn't get near it at all when he realized it wasn't a seal at all but an island!

In the early days the only way to go after a seal was by crawling on your stomach. We had a shield to keep out of sight from the seal. We also had a small *kamootik* to which the shield was attached, and it had a sharp point in front so that when the seal was near enough we would push the small *kamootik* hard and the sharp point would hit the seal. Even if a man crawled into water, he didn't care. He was after a seal and he didn't care if he got himself all wet. He had to have food to feed his family. That was how most of the men hunted seals.

Also when a person had caught a big animal, the women would have to drop their sewing for two or three days. If one woman kept on sewing when someone had caught a big animal, there was going to be one person in the family who would die; so everyone had to listen.

We had to take care of everything so that things would last a long time. All the harnesses of the dogs had to be cleaned good and dried again and again. The harnesses were sometimes full of dirt and dog shit. We had to take care of our clothes because sometimes they didn't last long. The children had to clean their own clothes. They would take the snow off their clothes and *kamiks* with a knife and dry them over a fire when they were ready to go to bed.

These were the things that the Eskimos did in the early days.

The old way of living

Told by
Aksayook Etoangat
aged 75
of Pangnirtung

I was born at Kikitaet. I grew up there. When I became a teenager we moved out of Kikitaet. We were going hungry there because we hadn't gone out on the ice in the fall. The ice wasn't yet frozen enough, so we couldn't hunt for food.

We didn't have any guns to hunt with; so we had to wait for seals beside their air holes. Very early in the mornings a man would wake every other man, shouting. He would shout that it was time to go hunt seals. The men would walk down to the bay and wait beside the seal holes for a seal to come up. They would try to get a seal that had lots of blood in it because blood is good for the people. When a spear or harpoon was used the seal had more blood in it, but if a gun was used most of the blood poured out of the seal. When the seal was harpooned or speared, the men plugged the hole which the harpoon had made with a walrus tusk. This is how they used to do in the old days to keep the blood from pouring out.

Later they would cut up the meat to take home for their family. They would save almost everything of the seal. Even the long intestines are good to eat when cooked.

Some men would catch quite a few seals, while some didn't catch any at all, but we all shared our food with one another. When all the men came home from their trips, and after they had settled down, the men who had caught seals would call all the people to come and eat together. All the people would get together and eat as much as they wanted. They always did this down at Kikitaet.

When the people ate they would have some meat, not very much because we had to save some for some other time, and they would also have some of the blood in place of tea because in those days we didn't have any tea or coffee to drink. If some people didn't want meat right there, they would save it and take it home to eat later on, but they would always have some of the blood from the seal to drink.

When the people had finished eating from the seal, the women would sew the part which the men had cut open, so that the blood that was left would not pour out of it. If the men caught more than one seal, they would take the skins off and take them, with the blubber, to the white man. The blubber was the only thing that helped the Eskimos have fire in the winter to cook their food; so they also kept some blubber for themselves.

Then the next day the men could go hunt seals again, to a different place this time. And this time the men who didn't get a seal the day before would try harder to catch one, but sometimes they still didn't catch any at all.

There was one white man down at Kikitaet who used to trade things for the sealskins. He would only trade for the skins that had blubber, and if the skins didn't have any blubber on them, he didn't give anything for them. When the Eskimos traded their skins, they would sometimes get white people's food in return, or some tobacco, or the men would get bullets.

Whenever the Eskimos got some seals they would give the white man some meat to eat, but instead the white man would put the meat into barrels so that, when the Eskimos couldn't go out hunting in the spring when the ice was breaking, or when it was fall and the water was just freezing — because that was when most of the people went hungry — he would give some meat to the families who didn't have any food.

When I left Kikitaet to a càmp called Edloogatyoot there were no people there; so there used to be a great number of seals. After I had been there for a while I left again to someplace else. I had my own dogs but I was afraid they might starve. The person I was with had left so I was all alone. I had a step-father but he was somewhere else, too. I used to go out hunting for seals; and sometimes I got seals and sometimes I didn't. It was always the same with everyone else.

In the spring when there were baby seals, I would catch them and also I would sometimes catch the mothers, but, because I was weak, I didn't get very many full grown seals. I would use a spear or a harpoon to catch a seal; it was always the best way. It was a good time to start feeding my dogs so that they wouldn't starve to death.

The thing one had to watch for was the ice breaking. Some of the ice was pretty thin and one really had to know about it.

When I was old enough to have a wife, I went to Padloping because they asked me to go over to get married to the girl they had picked for me. I lived there for fourteen years with my wife, and my three children were born at that camp.

When my wife became sick, we left Padloping by dog team and came to Pangnirtung, because this was the only place where there was a nurse to look after sick people. It was a very long trip, but I had to get my wife to the hospital here in Pangnirtung. There were no doctors or nurses or even white people in Padloping. We camped in Pangnirtung, and while I was there, I was asked to go to the hospital to work, but I couldn't understand English so I didn't go. Then the next day they asked for me again.

I started to work for the hospital and continued for almost twenty years. I worked for the first white nurse who came to Pangnirtung. My job was taking her to different camps to see if there were any sick people that had to see the nurse. We went from camp to camp. Some families would not be at their main camps. They would be out caribou hunting or somewhere else and we had to go after them and look for them. Sometimes we would find them and sometimes we didn't.

In the summer I used to hunt whales with some whalers, and when it was time to go back to work the nurse and I would go from camp to camp again, bringing to the hospital people who had TB. We were always kept busy through the years.

When we were in a boat going after the families that were out caribou hunting, I would sometimes take my time and hunt seals on the way. Most of the time I would catch a lot of seals and my boat would be full, then I would go on land and look for the families who were sick or had TB to bring back to the hospital. In early fall I would go out seal hunting so that I could feed my dogs so that they would be in good condition to go to each camp in the winter to find the people who needed to see the nurse.

If some people came to Pangnirtung to the hospital with their own dogs and didn't have any food to feed them, I would give them some food. And when I went to their camps to look for the people who were sick, the people would give some meat to feed my dogs, too. I would always go to the camps with the nurse with me.

Sometimes men used to go seal hunting at night. While they waited during the night, they would tie their legs together so that they wouldn't move because if they made the slightest sound the seal might not come up for air. All night long they would have their legs tied together waiting for the seal to come up. While they waited, they would float something on top of the water in the seal hole so that when a seal came up for air the men would know when to harpoon it. They would wait day and night without eating or drinking. All they did was wait for a seal to come up and were patient while waiting.

When the men had caught a seal, they would untie their legs and pull it up.

Men went out, too, with white shields to hide themselves so that the seals wouldn't see them coming. Some men didn't have a shield; so they had to crawl on the ice to go after the seals. It took a long time to get to the seal, but it was the only way to get the seals if you wanted to have meat.

Sometimes the men would like to move faster, but if the seal found out that there was something after him, he'd just go down the seal hole and wouldn't come up for hours; so the men had to go quite slowly if they wanted to catch it and take it home.

I was getting to know a lot of things when I became a teenager.

The people hunted for food and for clothes for their children. They tried hard to do so. People moved from camp to camp. They used to move freely because the North is where the Eskimos lived for a long time and it is their land.

When they went out to hunt, some didn't even have anything to hunt with or any other thing at all. They didn't have food with them because there was nothing to eat. The only time they'd eat was when somebody caught a seal. But they went out with nothing. There were a lot of men; so there was no doubt that one of them would get a seal or two. The men would be quite happy going home to their families with some meat for them to eat.

There were men who had lots of dogs and men who didn't have very many or maybe even none. But the men who had dogs had to get food for their dogs too. Sometimes they would save some blood from the seals and get their wives to boil it and add some water so that when the men had come home their dogs could have something to drink or eat.

We used to boil the blood with blubber, cut up into small pieces. After it had boiled we froze it, and the kids would take small pieces and eat it as if it was candy. I think it was even better than candies or chocolate bars. It was a treat to the kids. When we were kids, we always used to go visiting so that we could get some of the frozen blubber and blood. After we were given some we would go out and play.

We learned while we played. The weather was always very cold, but we had to get used to it because when we were old enough to go out hunting we'd be out all day even if it was very cold. So, we were out playing most of the time or maybe learning from our father. We learned how to build an igloo, or how to take over the dogs, or anything that a man has to know, and when our fathers thought that we were ready to go out with them they would let us go.

My father used to tell me things about hunting so that I would know how to hunt when I grew up. If I didn't listen to what my father had to tell me, I wouldn't know how to support myself or my family; so I had to learn while I was still a little boy. As I grew up I learned more and still I'm learning different things.

When I was old enough to hunt by myself, I tried everything that my father had taught me. I remember that my father used to go out almost every day to get food for us and skins to clothe us all, and I always wanted to do the same when I grew up. Our clothes were skins. The men were the ones who had to get the clothes for the family.

When we lived out of Pangnirtung we were always peaceful. There were no white people there and there were a few of us so we weren't hungry. We shared everything. Once a year we would go to Pangnirtung to trade sealskins or other skins to buy things we really needed at the camps and to buy some bullets, too. The bullets were more important than the other things because we needed them to hunt.

When we returned to our camp, we'd hunt or maybe go down to Kikitaet for a while, and down at Kikitaet there were no white people.

In winter we'd go out on dog teams, to hunt seals or other animals. In spring, when there were baby seals, the men went out and would get a lot of them. It was always the best time to hunt because the seals would be on the ice, napping or getting the sun on their backs. The men today still hunt when there are baby seals.

The water edge was very far from camp, and the only way to get there was to go by dog teams with the boats on the *kamootiks*. The whalers went down to the edge this way. The four whalers' boats were very heavy. The leader, Ookamak (Mr. Page), would say when to go and the others would obey him. We would camp down by the water.

When there wasn't a whale to be seen anywhere, the men would just hunt seals or baby seals. The white men would take the skins or the blubber alone. The skins that the white men didn't take, the Eskimos would use them to make clothes. We also had someone who would bring the seals we had caught back to our main camp for us.

At night we would take turns sleeping. There was always someone who watched at night to see if there was a sperm whale near. When the men were out whaling they were homesick and lonesome for their wives.

Sometimes the men would be out for many weeks when they were out after sperm whales.

When someone saw a whale, we would all go out on the water and go after it. Once we were the ones that caught the sperm whale, and when the big whale was going around, I was scared that we might capsize and drown. It was my first time sperm whaling, too. But later on it was a lot of fun and I wasn't scared anymore.

The whale would go down for quite awhile and would come up again. It would sometimes take us about four hours to bring it to surface.

After we had caught it we would pull it towards the ice. When finally we had killed the whale, we had to wait for the ice to break before we could go back to our main camp to work on the big sperm whale. We often waited on the edge a long time for the ice to break to bring the whale in.

The men were always working hard whenever a sperm whale had been caught. Most of the men rowed, but there were two men who didn't row with the others. They were the leaders of the boat. One was in the front looking out for small or big icebergs, and the other was at the tiller. Sometimes, every two days, they took turns on rowing.

The men took turns eating in the boat. They didn't all stop to eat at once. They wanted to keep going so they could reach land sooner, and they could rest when they had reached land; so they took turns eating. In the mornings, the men would have some white man's food, but the rest of the days they would have seal meat, cooked, or fried.

The women back home, when their husbands were out whaling, had to hunt for food themselves. They had their husbands' dogs and some harpoons and spears. They didn't have any men to look after them except the old men and boys, and they were either too old or too young to hunt; so the women hunted for food.

The women caught a lot of seals, too. They would even catch, maybe, four seals from the same seal holes. They had to know how to hunt just like the men; so if their husbands were out and never came back, the women could hunt for their families. They were always happy and having fun hunting while their husbands were out whaling.

It was hard work for all of the men who had gone whaling, but we had a lot of fun. We worked on the whale and would clean and wash all the boats before we could stop and hunt for ourselves. The boats had to be cleaned for the next time we went back for whales.

When summer came, we would then go out caribou hunting to get some skins to make our clothes and for some food to eat. When we had enough to make our clothes, we would go back to our main camps.

The same year, in the fall, again there were whaling boats waiting for a whale to come; so if there was a whale, they'd go after it. It was very cold, but they were waiting for one to come. They didn't use a motor because there were no motors in those days. They used only paddles to run the boats.

The men who were in the boats didn't go after the sperm whales   50 because they had to but because they wanted to. They were always happy to go out whaling. They took turns sleeping, and also they would have to cook their own food and tea. After they had eaten they would then go after a whale. Sometimes they would go to one of the islands and wait for a sperm whale, and sometimes there were only two boats to go.

When the men had come back from hunting the women would be waiting for them by the water, and as soon as the boats were going close to shore the women would help pull the boats further inland. Sometimes, some of the men were still in the boats when the others were pulling the boats further inland.

When we couldn't go out by boat or by dog team because the ice was too frozen for boats but still not frozen enough for dog teams, we were going to go hungry, but there was always a tongue of the whale that was still left, and we had some of it. The tongue was the one thing that didn't go bad for quite a while while the rest of the meat was going bad.

After a while some men went for a walk up to the hills, and, when they were on top of the hill, they could see the ice and realized that the ice was frozen enough to travel on, and they were so happy. All the people were so happy for this good news when they heard about it; so they went hunting that day. They brought their boats, harpoons, spears, hooks, paddles, and other things that they needed when they went hunting.

That night they returned with seals they had caught. The people were happy for this. Almost every time the men went hunting, they'd catch seals, mustache seals, and other sea animals, and, as the people had food again, it seemed as if they had never been hungry. The men would go out every day and bring back food every night. Everybody was very happy again and so were the children. They had food to eat once more, and they were not going to go hungry for a few months.

Only the older men could go down to the floe edge because one really had to know how to hunt down there, and it was quite dangerous. We, the teenagers, used to go down to meet the older men when they were coming home so that we could take over their dog teams and bring them home for the men. The men were happy to let us take over because this way was also a way to learn how to take charge of the dogs.

If we went out with some men when they were going hunting, they would teach us how to hunt as if we were their own sons. Not all of us liked going with our own fathers. For example when my older brother didn't go out hunting, I would go with someone else so I could learn more. The men were always glad to teach the young boys how to hunt.

Of the sperm whale, the best part to eat is the *muktuk* ("whale skin"). I think it is even better than the white whale's skin, because even when white whales had been caught, the people kind of forgot about them when a sperm whale was caught. The people just love to eat the skin of the sperm whale. I mean, I'm not saying that the white whale's skin isn't good. It's just that the sperm whale's skin is a lot better.

Whenever a sperm whale had been caught the Eskimos would cut up

the whale *muktuk* and put it in sealskin bags, which they made especially to store blubber or meat to keep it from going bad, or they would put the *muktuk* into wooden barrels. The people always kept the meat or other things in sealskin bags or in wooden barrels. Even if the meat or *muktuk* became smelly it was good to eat. It was always good to eat as long as it didn't really go bad, but it is never poison.

When somebody had speared a sperm whale and the rope broke, everyone was always sorry because they couldn't catch it anymore. It was always hard to catch the whale after the rope had broken; so everyone was always sorry when this happened.

This was the life the Eskimos led in the old days, and now they no longer use this way of living. They now have a new way of living.

The things that went around

Told by
Paulosie Qappik
aged 65
of Pangnirtung

We were living in a camp called Olik when I started remembering the things that went around and the things I did.

We were always waiting for my father to come home from hunting when we were all hungry.

In the spring we went down to Kikitaet, past Kagitook. We were still at Kikitaet when fall came. When spring came again, men went down to the floe edge to hunt seals, but my father didn't need to go with the others. In the fall, when all the family had been hungry, my father had gone down to the floe edge, had seen two whales, and had caught both of them. That was when my father was getting older. He had put some meat away, but later the dogs got the meat, and we all felt pretty bad and pretty mad at them.

After a few months, we started packing up our things. My grandfather and all his family were coming with us to go someplace else. We had fish and walrus for food. We gave the walrus skins to the white man.

Then the time came when we went hungry again, but we just stayed in our camp because the ice was too thin to travel on it. When it froze up good, we headed south, and on the way we waited beside seal holes for seals to come up for air. We caught a few seals. Then we moved to a place where a white man lived, where there were some supplies we could buy if we needed them. My parents decided to live there.

In those days we were always poor and hungry. We used to go out to hunt for only a day sometimes; even now people go out for a day or so, but

most people have forgotten how to hunt. Nowadays they only depend on the things that the white men bring to the North. We had hard times in those days.

In the summertime we had to make our own boats out of sealskins. We paddled from place to place. There were no motors in those days; so we only used sails and paddles. Sometimes it was dangerous to go out in our boats when there was going to be a storm, but just the same, we had fun hunting. Often we were out for caribou for four days or more.

Sometimes our clothes were too hot because they were made of skin. In the summer our clothes ripped very easily, and when they got wet from us, they had a very bad smell because they were skins. When the white man came up North, we got cloth and some material to make clothes, and it was an improvement. Our children wore skins for clothing, too, but now we do not hunt very often to get our clothes because now there is a store where we can buy them. It was hard to hunt in those days when we didn't have a gun and bullets, but now it is a lot easier.

I started remembering in the days when people still used the *kayak*. They'd go out in their *kayak*, and when they had caught a seal, even if it was bleeding, they'd put it inside the *kayak* to take home for their family.

When the men caught a seal, they'd cut it up in small pieces, and also they didn't waste the blood; they didn't throw it away but saved it, too. It was always fun when my father came from seal hunting. We were happy when he had caught seals. The rest of the kids and I were happy then.

I had two wives. The first one died when I was still young, and then I married again at the age of forty-nine, but she also died. Now I am sixty-four years old and no longer hunt. I'm no longer wearing caribou or sealskin clothes but white man's clothes. The white man is helping me with food, and I now live with my daughter and her family because I don't have a wife.

This is a story which I heard from my mother years ago.

There were two camps in Kakatoona, The son of Kookoopaloognoa was taken to another land away from them. The people who took this boy killed him. Kookoopaloognoa said that he was going after the people who took his son; so the following summer he started towards their camp, alone.

When he got there he found the house of a person who was blind. When he saw his son's parka hanging inside his tent, he asked whose caribou parka it was, and up in the back he saw something wrapped in sealskins. Kookoopaloognoa started poking at it with a stick. He felt something but no cry came from it.

When he lifted the sealskins he saw flesh falling out of the skins, but still no cry came from it. Then he found out that this thing that was wrapped in sealskins was the body of his son which the people had hidden in the back of the house where the blind person lived.

The men of this camp were out seal hunting at the time Kookoopaloognoa arrived at their camp; so he went down to where the men were, and when he had reached them he said, "You men, I am the father of the boy you killed. I am only one, and I'm also very weak, but are you able to fight me? You are many but I am one." One of the men threw his spear at Kookoopaloognoa, but he took his bow and arrows and started killing them. There were quite a few men against one, but they couldn't touch Kookoopaloognoa.

After the men were dead, Kookoopaloognoa went back to the camp where the men's wives were, and he made a very big house for the women. Before he left them to go on to his own camp, he put all the women in the house and told them they would live there now.

After that day, Kookoopaloognoa was a very important man to the people in his camp.

This story is about a family who lived in a camp called Keemeesoo.

There was a grandfather and a grandmother in the camp. The grandfather had a female dog who had puppies. He made every puppy a harness. The only grown dog was the mother of the pups, but still the grandfather was going to go out on the *kamootik*. He tied the puppies onto the *kamootik* and whipped them to go. He was going away without letting the others know, but the others found out and followed after him.

The grandmother couldn't keep up with the others and got mad; so she stamped her feet on the ice, and the ice split in half, and the people started floating on the ice. They didn't know where they were heading to, but they finally landed on Greenland. They decided to live there; so that is how people started living in Greenland.

The years I started remembering

Told by
Josephee Sowdloapik
aged 65 from
Kekertukdjuak

Years ago, when I was a small boy, I remember my parents going camp to camp. I remember, too, that I was a very bad boy. In those days, when we were kids, we used to fight a lot and we were very bad boys. And whenever I got in a fight I would scratch somebody, and would discover afterwards that there were bits of skin under my nails. When I was a boy I wouldn't do anything but fight. We used to be like that when we were living in Kekertukdjuak. We kids used to fight a lot when we were together.

I used to be afraid to be alone. Once, when I was alone, I shot some caribou. I started walking and didn't want to stop until I met people because I might be caught by something that wasn't human. Once when a friend and I were walking over to the other side of the place where we were camping, we saw a ghost. We became afraid. We had a gun with us and I wanted my friend to shoot at the ghost. I was so afraid that I started crying. We thought that the ghost we were seeing was the ghost of my friend's grandfather.

We used to have a camp near Pangnirtung and would race to Nasuya. Once we saw some tracks, we thought they were not a person's tracks, so we ran to our camp. We were so afraid that I began to cry. We thought that they were ghost's tracks. Then somebody went to look for them and when he came back he told us that they were only goose tracks!

When I was a man I wasn't afraid of water. I had a wife then, and I used to go out hunting when the fiord was just like a soft snow. Sometimes

I used to fall through into the water and get up again. Those days I was a very fine young man. Even my *kamootik* used to go underwater, but a mighty me pulled it up from the water. I used to be happy to do that. When my *kamootik* went underwater, so did my dogs. When this happened I often went home without them because I was in a very bad situation. Once I saw my things in a box, floating away, so I jumped into the water and got the box. Some people wouldn't do what I've done.

I used to walk on ice pans. Once I got scared by a whirlpool. I was on an ice pan and floating on the water. While I was floating I reached a whirlpool. I could not do anything. I did not know what to do that time. I went on floating on the water and I just sat there and did nothing. Suddenly I realized that I was saved from the whirlpool. That was the first time I got scared.

I used to be the fastest runner, nobody ever beat me. The men who went walking with me were always way behind. When I reached our camp I could not even see the others because they were so far away from me. I used to walk very fast when I was young, but now I'm too old to walk like I used to. One day, my son and I went to Ekalljuak to live there. We had many dogs; our dogs were very healthy and fast. While I was riding on my *kamootik* I saw that one side of my *kamootik's* braid was missing, and so I ran around to get it. I was running so fast that my leg broke!

Years ago I was out camping with my cousin near to our own camp. There were a lot of foxes around, but there was one thing we did not have.

We did not have any tobacco to smoke. My cousin wanted to smoke as much as I did. He took off his shirt while we were walking, and we smoked from it. It smelled like an old wet cloth. As we walked we realized that it was all gone; he did not have his shirt on and there was not a piece left. It smelled so awful. I never wanted to smoke again.

Several days later, at our camp, I thought of going to Pangnirtung. So, off I went to Pangnirtung. While I spent a day there I caught a very bad cold and did a lot of coughing. When I coughed it smelled like the shirt I had been smoking. My lungs got bad from the material I was smoking.

I used to look for tobacco on the sea shore and once found some very old tobacco. I was very happy that I was going to smoke again. When I finished smoking I got very hot and my face was sweating. I used to like tobacco a lot. I even used to put my old dirty pants in my mouth. I couldn't live without tobacco before I quit smoking.

I would like to tell you another story about how much I wanted to smoke. We were out camping, as usual. I was inside our tent with my wife. I told my wife to look for tobacco outside our tent. So, she went out to look for some. I knew there was only caribou meat outside our tent. When my wife got back, she had nothing in her hands and told me that she couldn't find any tobacco. So I started to cry. My wife just laughed at me.

Years passed and I had plenty of tobacco to smoke. I enjoyed myself and sometimes threw some away to pay for my desire for tobacco. That is the end of my desire for tobacco.

Once while I was hunting, I saw a caribou. I did not have bullets or stones to kill the caribou, so I ran after it. I got to the caribou and jumped on it and held on to its horns. The caribou tried to drop me down, but I would not fall. I had a knife with me, so I pulled my knife out and cut the neck of the caribou while I was still on its back.

I used to go hunting for baby seals in spring when there were many of them. The snow was very soft, and I got many of them. I was a happy hunter when I was young. There used to be many animals. We have killed many. Even Pangnirtung used to have many animals, but now there's no more around. After my grandfather died I kept his dogs. I killed many animals when I had dogs.

Many years ago when I was a teenager, we were out hunting caribou. We killed many caribou. One time I looked back and saw a caribou getting up from the ground. So I went running after it with my dog tied to my hand. The caribou was getting tired but I was not tired. My dog went after the caribou and killed it.

Once I went to Pangnirtung, and while I was on my way there my dogs got very hungry and tired. When I arrived in Pangnirtung my brother-in-law fed my dogs and they were full again. I was very happy that my dogs were going to be fast again. When I was ready to leave Pangnirtung, one of my dogs seemed to get very sick and nearly died. After I thought that my dogs were going to be fast, one of them died. Nearly all of them died; soon there were only three of them left. So I

walked home and left my dog team, because I was faster than the three dogs I had left.

When autumn came, and there were some whales near our camp. We used to have fun throwing our spears at the whales. Sometimes we used to throw small stones and see who could throw farthest. And I was the best and threw farthest. Many men used to hunt whales those days.

Once there was a lady, who went to visit to another land with her daughter. The lady was mixing wolf's brain and man's brain. She told her daughter not to tell anyone what she was doing. She was mixing them together to make the people die. The little girl did not want to do this, but she had to listen to her mother; so she sang a song when she was alone. This is the song which she sang. "Oh, Mother, you are mixing a wolf's brain to make the people die, and you do not want me to tell them; so I will not tell." That is the song she sang.

Kassuk was a young man, and he liked to shoot at the chimneys. One day while he was in his boat some men were trying to kill him. Kassuk ran away so fast that the men could not come near him. He was very far away, and suddenly he saw a man who ran away from other men too. The man Kassuk met was very poor. Kassuk said to the man, "Now I'm trying to do the things that I used to be afraid of." And he killed the man.

66

Once there was a man who went hunting. He sang as he rode away on his dog team. This is the song which he sang:

"I'm riding on my dog team,
I've got muscles;
When I try to get off,
I get off."

Once there was a blind man who lived all alone with his mother. The blind man knew how to use his spear. One day a polar bear came to their camp and his mother told the blind man to kill the polar bear with his spear; so the blind man threw his spear at the polar bear and killed it. But, the blind man didn't know that he had killed the polar bear because he wasn't able to see. His mother kept the polar bear's meat in secret, and only gave her son a very little meat for his supper.

It was getting summer and the whales were around again. Then the blind man said, "Let me see, let my eyes see again." Then two geese flew to him, picked him up and dropped him into a lake, and this made him see again. Off he went back to his camp. When he arrived there, he saw his mother cleaning a polar bear skin. His mother said, "Some men who were here left this polar bear skin." He knew she told a lie.

There were a lot of whales near their camp. They went to the place where the whales were, and the man tied the spear rope around his mother's waist and threw the spear at one of the whales and hit one. Then he let go of the rope and off went his mother right behind a white whale.

This is a song which used to be sung years ago. It goes something like this:

"Didn't you hear that he killed an animal for the dogs to eat?
Didn't you hear?
Go gather some plants for your bed."

Kowjayook was a very poor girl. She lived with the dogs. She was very poor. She ate with the dogs when the dogs had their meals. When the moon came out of the sky every evening, she would sing, "There is the moon; there is my brother up there." The man in the moon made her big, and someone began shouting from the camp that Kowjayook had grown big.

The old men of the camp then asked, "Should she grow so big? Hang her by her nose." But when Kowjayook grew big she began to sing, and the people ran away from her. Kowjayook spoke, "The person who used to be mean to me, I now take him; the person who I used to be so scared of, I now take him; the person who used to hang me by my nose, I now take him, too." And all these people she took and she killed.

68

There was a small child who was living with a grandmother. The grandmother was tired of sewing the child's clothes, and one day told the child to go to a lake and get into it. When the child got into the lake he turned into a seal. He could see the people on the land playing. They went out in their *kayaks* and started following the boy who had turned into a seal. While they were following the seal they went so far out from land that they couldn't see land anymore. It became windy and soon a storm came. The *kayaks* started to tip over and some of the men drowned and were lost.

The little seal changed back into a boy again and sat on top of the water and said, "I want another storm to come." And another storm came, and all but one of the *kayaks* were lost. The only person who was left was Keeveoq. He had a small bird inside his *kayak*. Keeveoq was the only person alive after the storm while the others were all dead and lost. He paddled to the land and was all alone. He would see people around but they were spirits or ghosts.

For twelve years Keeveoq was away from home. He was getting old. When he got close to home his wife recognized him, and she sang the song that she used to sing whenever her husband came home from hunting. It goes something like this, "Keeveoq comes home again, aseegee aseegee-seegee aseegeeseegee."

Once there was a crow who married a female fox. He was told that if he smelled something to pretend he didn't smell it. The fox started to move around, and soon she started smelling like you wouldn't believe. Then the crow asked, "Where's that smell coming from?" And that was the end between the crow and the fox.

The crow soon married again, to a goose. The crow was told that the goose goes to far away places, but the crow just said, "That doesn't matter." He was told that when geese get tired they land on water and rest. But the crow just said he would wait until they started flying again. Soon the geese landed on water to rest and the crow flew above waiting for them to fly again. The geese took their time resting, and the crow was getting tired. He got so tired that he finally fell down to the sea, and that was the end of the crow.

One time when I was hunting I saw a seal. I took my shield and went closer to it. The seal was staring at me. I threw my shield down and waved at the seal; I did not want to be stared at by that seal. The next day I went hunting again; I carried my gun. Not long out I soon saw the seal. The seal came up from his hole; my legs were trembling with fear. I almost started to cry. I just shot at the seal and left it. Then I went to tell my father what happened. And as soon as we got back to the seal's hole, we saw the seal was still there, and it was dead, too. I was very proud to kill a seal for the first time.

I was a good hunter when I was a teenager. One day I was hunting and I caught a baby seal by its flippers. The mother was trying to get her baby so I killed the mother seal, too. I tried to pull up the mother seal but I could not. She was so heavy that my arms seemed to tear. So, I let my dogs get her out of the hole. I went to Pangnirtung when there were many baby seals around. I killed one on my way to Pangnirtung so I could get some tobacco.

One day I shot four seals. I pulled the seals all the way to my camp. I used to be faster than my dogs. Once when I was hunting I saw a seal on a fiord; I went closer to it. While I was walking my feet went in the water. The snow was very thin and soft. Three times I've been underwater, but I never died. I used to be a very quick man and wasn't afraid of water.

We used to have camp near Pangnirtung. There were many, many animals around. There used to be many seals at the water's edge in Pangnirtung. One time, the seals were followed by killer whales. The killer whales were very fast. When the tide went out many seals were left on the seashore. We brought our ships to the shore, and we killed them. We used to do that a long time ago. We used to watch the whales when they were far away from the land. My friend once told me to shoot at the whales and I shot one, even when they were very far from the land. One time I shot a caribou swimming in the lake far away from land. Another time, my friend wanted me to shoot a seal which was very far away, so I took the rifle and shot at the seal, and I managed to kill it.

Once, in fall, it was windy and I'd heard that there was a cave near that was good for shelter when it was windy. So I went there by boat and when we got there it was still windy; so we tied our boat to the rocks and we were ready to go to sleep in the cave. When I woke up, I went out to see if our boat was there, but when I got to the place where we tied it, it wasn't there. I started to look for it, and later on I found it far away from where we stayed overnight.

This is the end of my stories, and all of them are true. I used to be a brave man.

Things from a long time ago and nowadays

Told by
Malaya Akulujuk
aged 61
from Kikitaet

This is how things were a long time ago, before we were born.

The people used to go out hunting when the ice was breaking up. In the springtime they used to go out camping, and they would not return until summer was over. They used to go home when the water was still good for *kayaks*.

Up there where we used to camp, the seals were really huge. Eskimos used to make boats out of their skins. They made *kayaks* also. The only difference between Pangnirtung's seals and Nutseelik's seals is that a Nutseelik seal's eyes are really big and they have crossed eyes.

We had our own way of doing things. We told stories that were told to us by older people. And, sometimes, we can still do the things that were done a long time ago, when we have to do them. The older people always tell their grandchildren stories and the things that they used to do.

This story was told by Kowyayook.

When he was a little boy he was very poor, and he used to sleep outside with the dogs. The only thing that kept him warm was those dogs. As he grew up and knew more things that were going on around him, he started to draw away from other people.

One night when he was sleeping with the dogs, he was touched on his shoulder, and he woke up right away. He looked around and saw a man. He beckoned Kowyayook to follow. He followed him and they stopped beside a big rock, and there he told the boy many things that he didn't know. One thing the man told him was that he could give him power.

Then he said he had to slap Kowyayook hard, many times, to give him strength. So he slapped him many times and, when he had been slapped many times, Kowyayook started to feel stronger; he said that he could feel the strength coming, and it was true. Kowyayook was told to lift three rocks of different sizes. He lifted all the three rocks. He was overjoyed to have that power and strength.

Meanwhile, people were looking everywhere for Kowyayook but they couldn't' find him. Kowyayook and the man returned to the camp, and they met the people when they got there. The man then told Kowyayook to go to Nanokoma, the leader of the people at the camp, and tell him to come to him. But Nanokoma wouldn't come. The people started to draw away from Kowyayook, and they were really scared of him. He had never acted this way before, and they didn't know what had happened to him. The people ran away from him and he ran after them. As he ran after them he said, "Kowyayook who was very poor is now coming!"

The people who had been mean to Kowyayook hid, but he caught one woman. He said, "You are the most cruel lady I have ever known, and for that I'm going to make you pay for the bad things you did to me." And Kowyayook broke all her bones, and he took out her eyes and put them in backwards. He let her suffer as he had suffered all his life. He wanted them all to know the suffering he had known since he was a small boy.

When he was old enough to marry he got himself three wives. He was a good hunter; so his wives didn't run out of meat. His first wife was a parka maker, and his second wife made pants and underwear for him. His third wife made *kamiks* for him. He felt rich then. He used to be a good storyteller, and he told that story to others, but it is never the same story when other people tell it.

I was born in Kikitaet. I didn't have parents; so I lived with my foster parents. I was born when the war was going on and the people didn't have enough food to eat. We used to get white people's food from Sowmeanie.

There was a white man in Kikitaet. We used to call him Mapatak. He had a white man's name but I forget it. He used to take care of me though he was a white man; he used to give me white man's food. I used to share my own meals with him when my foster mother asked me to. He used to cry when I did that; he was very thankful. He didn't want to take our food, but we told him that he could eat with us. That was when there was a war.

Mapatak was really happy and he sweated a lot. He wore false teeth that didn't fit anymore. He was very skinny. He was looking forward to getting a letter from home. Three years passed when finally the ship came in and he got a letter from his wife and his first son. His second son had died in the war. He and his daughter went to our place to read his letter.

We were still living in Kikitaet when people started to live in

Pangnirtung. There was a ship that used to come to Kikitaet, but the ship caught on fire. Joanasee Dialla's father used to have a ship, too, and it used to come here in summertime. Since then white people have been coming here.

It isn't too long ago that I was a teenager. We were told to look forward to our future and what to expect out of life. Also, they used to say that we would be living more like white people, and it's true. Our kids will be used to this new life. We have to prepare our kids. Children, don't forget the real Eskimo way of life, and tell your kids the wonderful Eskimo stories. Tell them stories that happened a long time ago.

I hope nobody forgets the things that happened a long time ago. We had a better way to live than what we are living now. Life was magnificent.

I was born in a camp which we call Kikitaet sometime before or after the days of December. I was born in winter, in an igloo, the time when women had their babies alone, the time nobody believed there was a true God or had ever heard of the Lord Jesus Christ.

I remember when I was a very small girl, my mother carried me in her *amoutik*. We went out on the *kamootik*. When I wanted to pee, I was afraid to go if it was a very cold day.

When my mother carried me in her *amoutik,* we went over to Oomanayoak for a visit. A white man who was the leader over in Kikitaet was with us on the trip. There were a herd of caribou on the ice so my father, Armarlik, and Kooloo, and the white man went after the caribou while my mother was left to watch the team of dogs.

Because the dogs wanted to go after the caribou themselves, they disobeyed their master and went after the caribou herd. When the dogs ran off, my mother didn't know what to do and was afraid. She couldn't stop the dogs, and anyway they were too far away to be stopped; so she decided to start walking toward the igloo which was some miles away. She started to cry, thinking that somehow, from someplace, someone would stop the dogs. She wanted to cry out loud but because she knew I would be afraid she just cried to herself.

Then a miracle happened. The dogs stopped as though someone had stopped them. It's because my mother had trusted that somewhere there was a greater person than the people on earth.

Things that we used to do in the old days that no longer exist

Told by
Katsoo Eevic
aged 78
of Pangnirtung

78

Not long after she arrived at the igloo the white man also returned. He said that he could not eat raw caribou like the Eskimos but would eat after it had been cooked. He said he would go over to Oomanayoak for Taenah who had been his cook before Taenah married.

Later, when my parents returned to Kikitaet from Oomanayoak, they saw that the people had changed from their old ways of life into bad and evil ways and worshipped a false god they called Sanah. My mother wanted the people to turn back. So in the summer my mother got some women together to make caribou clothes. The clothes were at least two times as big as the ones Eskimos wore, or maybe bigger than anybody could use on earth. My mother cut out the patterns and the women sewed them together. They made everything, the parka, the *kamiks*, the mittens, the pants, in fact the whole works. After they finished, everything was thrown into the water because that is what my mother wanted them to do. They made those clothes so that they could throw them into the water and no longer be followers of this god.

But, after this incident, the people remained evil. My mother had tried to tell them to turn from their evil ways but because she was a woman they didn't listen. When my father helped her then the people listened. There were witch doctors in those days and they, too, gave up their witchcraft to follow Sanah. The witch doctors I remember were Ookaetok, Inumah, and Alevattah, and a woman whose name was Ashoeetok. I never knew others besides these four. Since I was a small girl people have turned from their old way of believing that there was a god that helped them in hunting, a god that was on earth; one that the witch doctors saw.

Years ago when I was a little girl in Kikitaet there used to be a minister there. There were houses there which belonged to the Americans where this minister had his church services. We also learned how to write from him. The minister was called Ilatakao. Ilakakao taught the Eskimos in the house where the leaders lived. He used to teach my mother, Alikatootook, and others besides her, like Atsianak. My parents used to do arithmetic, too. The younger kids were taught separately. I still remember some of the things we learned, like the Eskimo syllabics and ABC's. I can write the ABC's but when it comes to reading sentences, forget it, because I don't know how. I also learned the numbers and I know them now.

After Ilatakao left us there came another white man who took his place. We were always thankful for Ilatakao's teaching us even if any others didn't want to learn. There were all together three men who came up North. I hardly remember the very first one who came. He had come here to teach the Eskimos when they didn't believe in the Christ. He had been the very first man to come up North. My mother told me that she and Nueejaot were just a few who learned from this man. Right now Nueejaot is still living; she lives down in Frobisher Bay. My mother and Nueejaot and others, Neengeogarpik and Kilabuk, taught the others how to write in Eskimo.

I remember, too, that a white man who made barrels wanted to teach me English but I didn't know if I wanted to learn, so every time he came over to our house, I'd go out.

My parents didn't have any other children besides me, so every evening we'd sit and practice writing and did arithmetic together at home. They didn't know very much but they learned a lot more than I did.

I remember, too, when Etuangat was born. He is now getting old. He was born in the spring the time a small ship was stuck in the ice down at Kikitaet. My mother was the midwife. I was there when Etuangat was born because I didn't have anybody to look after me. I remember the ice became very black from the ship.

I think that was the time a white man whom the Eskimos called Koopealeesak came. He was going to be the barrel maker here in Kikitaet. Wood to make barrels came by ship. These barrels were going to be used for oil from seal blubber. The oil was to be sent out.

The white man, Koopealeesak, was left to the work while his boss went over to Oomanayoak to visit. But instead of working, Koopealeesak stole liquor that belonged to his boss and was drinking heavily. He drank so much that he passed out and froze to death. I remember when we found him in the house, frozen, his bubbles still coming out of his mouth. We left him in the house so when his boss returned from his trip, he could do whatever he wished to do with Koopealeesak's body.

Before the boss returned, my father went out seal hunting for two days and left my mother and me alone in our house. While I was asleep, she heard someone at the door and saw that it was someone who looked frozen. My mother tried to wake me up but I would not wake up; so she went to the door and tried to open it, but she couldn't because the man was holding the door shut. My mother became afraid and didn't know what to do. After a little while, the man started walking back. We heard his footsteps and then, all of a sudden, couldn't hear them, and he vanished into thin air. I think my mother saw the ghost of Koopealeesak that night. She told me that story the next day.

Because my parents had no child other than me, we went out of camp very often in the winter time. Over at Oomanayoak my mother had an older sister; so we went there very often. I remember those days when we used to go there. The people I remember that were kids were Nootaga and Tojatoga. There were others, too, like Tonicjoolik, but they were a lot younger than me. There were other kids, but I don't quite remember them.

I remember seeing the porch that Onarpik made out of earth and mud. They were poor people. They had kids, too, Kilabuk and others. I remember seeing Ookijoasee, Oojagak, and Noah's grandmother, and also Aseevak, Kalayook's husband. Aseevak was my mother's first husband, and before she came to my father, she had had another husband also named Aseevak. They were separated when he was drowned. She then married my father. Only when death came to my father were they separated.

There were a few of us who went up to Nutseelik. We circled the lake up there. Kakik and his wife and their only child, a daughter who later died from starvation, were also with us. I can still see a large herd of caribou on the side of the hills. We were in a boat and, because we didn't have motors in those days, we were very slow as we only paddled or used a sail. The herd of caribou were a very nice sight to see as they walked on the hillsides. Some of them were male caribou with very large antlers. They were walking towards the old camp.

We landed someplace around there. Kakik became sick with fever. He was in another boat with some others. There were two boats. There were Kakik, Koopalik, Tasoogna, and Akootoo. I think Akootoo was the same age as Atsayook. They were first to land. So later on we started out again. Kakik was getting over with the fever, only this time his sister, Akootoo, came down with it. We started back to our camp when another became sick. This time it was Atsayook.

When the white man first came, before there were many people living in Pangnirtung, my mother worked for the white man, cleaning house for him. She had other women to help her with the cleaning if there was too much to do. I had known since I was a little girl that my mother had had quite a few stomach aches and, with those aches, she'd black out. Sometimes I thought that she was going to die. But, while I was thinking that she was going to die, she reached an old age.

83   Because my mother thought she was not going to live long, she taught

me how to make things like clothes for my family while I was a little girl. I tried to learn. I'd do all the things my mother wanted me to. Then when I got married, I sewed sealskins for the *kayak*. I could never have done that if I hadn't learned from my mother. I'm always thankful to her for teaching me those things that a woman should know.

Here is a story which I heard from my mother years ago.

When she was a young girl, while her parents were out hunting for a day or so with other parents from our camp, a polar bear came to the camp. There were small dogs outside barking at it. My mother had an axe ready in her hands just in case the bear tried to attack. The younger kids fed him with blubber by throwing it outside to the bear. While the bear ate, the kids poked at him with a knife they tied to a long stick.

My mother thought that if the bear slapped the igloo, the igloo would break into pieces, but luckily the bear didn't do that. When the bear stood up on his hind legs, my mother was afraid, and so she lit pieces of paper and threw them at the bear. When the bear opened his mouth she could see it was very black and dark inside. My mother was so afraid that she didn't know she was afraid!

Then the bear left them and, when it didn't return, the other kids went out of their homes, pulling behind a boy that was too nervous to stand up on his own feet. My mother tried to warn them not to go out because the bear might be somewhere near. True enough, the bear was near the camp, but now he was asleep because his tummy was full of blubber.

When the parents headed home they found polar bear tracks. They hurried home to check their children and found they were all unharmed. That was the very first time my mother was really afraid in her life.

When I became a teenager I went caribou hunting for the last time with my parents, up to Nutseelik. That's before I was married. After I married I never went back to Nutseelik to go caribou hunting. My father wasn't well enough to go far away places anymore.

I remember, after I had a husband, a few of us went out on my father's boat with Taena, Nookigna's husband, up to Eshooeetoo and Meeloogealik to go caribou hunting. After the time we went up to Meeloogealik I was expecting to have my first baby. We went back to our camp and in the fall my first daughter was born. We named her Annie. I started having other children. Now Annie is getting older and even her children are grown-ups and some even have children of their own. I still love my children as if they were small. Even if I cannot give my love away very deeply.

I lost a child and was in a shock for awhile. I went into another shock when my daughter, Ooleepeeka, went from one man to another. I didn't want her to do this. Maybe that's why I went into shock one summertime up beside Nutseelik. There were a few of us up there. All my children were with us except my son, Sakee, who was getting married. Also my grandchild, Lye, my daughter Annie's and her husband, Owyaloo's son, were with us that time. My husband prayed for me, and I, too, said prayers because I didn't want to lose our Lord God. I was thankful I wasn't going out of my mind. I was in the same situation of shock when my father left us, when he died of old age. There were a lot of people dying that summer.

While we were camping one time near Saveajuk, my husband became sick and said that he might not last long and he didn't know how we were going to be if he left us. The mustache sealskins on our boat were peeling off and we had to repair it. My husband couldn't help us because he was sick, but he told us what to do.

After we had finished mending that boat, a large boat with motors arrived with Jameesie and his father, Alevattah. Our small boat was tied to theirs and we headed towards Pangnirtung. Just before we reached land, my husband, Eevic, got worse but was still aware of what was happening. When we reached Pangnirtung we went to the hospital, where my husband was put to bed. I was to be there, too, as the nurses told me to. Not long after we arrived at the hospital, my husband no longer breathed.

I went out to go to my tent. My daughter, Annie, told me to stay with her in her tent so I would be near her when I needed her, but I really didn't need help because I wasn't in shock like I was when my daughter, Ooleepeeka, was going from one man to another. There were lots of white people who helped me with food and clothes after my husband was gone. I was thankful for them, too, and still I'm thankful.

Except for the child that I lost, none of my children have died yet.   86

We shall always do things, different things, now and for as long as we shall live. Right now we expect different things to happen. I want to be with and do things with my dear children and their children who now can think for themselves, and tell them about the things that we used to do in the old days that no longer exist.

Here on earth we were put, and we shall be the people we were before, but this time we will have something to wait for when we die. There are no strangers here on earth. We were made by the one true God who watches over us. He made Adam and Eve who were the first people on earth. He made the earth which we stand on. The houses we live in, which we built near white men, are nice and warm, and I'm very grateful for having a warm place to live.

For me, my children grew up too fast. The one child I love most in my family is Jaco, my son. I love him very much. Now he has a disease, but when he was a teenager he used to do lots of things. He was rough on himself and now he cannot do anything. Sometimes he can hardly walk. My other son, Sakee, was also sick for awhile but, because there is medicine to help him get back to health, he is well. He still feels pain in his neck but not very much. He had hurt himself while he was on his ski-doo. I thank him for giving me seal meat whenever he gets any. His older brother, Jaco, used to go out hunting for food for his family and for himself when he was still well. Also my grandsons, Jaco's children, will go out hunting for food if their father cannot go out himself and they, too, bring back food for us all.

Manasa, my youngest son, also hunts for food; he gives me some, too, and I thank him for being so thoughtful. Before he came to Pangnirtung, he used to live with his wife's parents. Sometimes I wanted to see him but I couldn't because he was so far away. When his wife died I asked him to come to me and he did, without any questions. I was thankful he had listened to me when I wanted him with me.

I have been helped a lot of times and I am thankful very much. After my husband died and left me with Manasa and Iga, still small children, I was helped by other people. Now my children are grown-ups and have children of their own.

After my husband died, I had good given to me by others. After a while my step-brother asked me to come to Pangnirtung to live and so I did. But later on I wanted to go back. When my son, Jaco, went there to hunt caribou I returned with him, and when I recognized the land I was so happy to see it again.

Now I don't think about the past too much because I should be happy where I am, in Pangnirtung, because that is how the Lord God wants us to be, happy.

My grandmother used to tell me stories when I was a girl. My grandmother's name was Tookah. She said her grandchild got everything she wanted from her grandmother. I'm going to tell some of the stories I still remember.

Once there were two people who were the first to hear music. They told other people what they had heard. They said that the music went something like this.

Dareo, dareo, dareo;
Kalee, kalee, kalee.

They didn't know anything about music.

Someone heard music again, and told other people that the music went like this.

Tidlitagavit, tidlitgavit;
Koopialalu.

They couldn't understand what the music was about.

I've heard that there were people who hunted whales a long time ago from their *kayaks*. They would surround the whales near to the land. Once, an old woman, with her hands under her pants, watched the men who tried to kill whales. Someone said, "Put your hands under the *kayaks* instead! Ay, ay, ay, ay." Then another one said, "I'm so afraid of whales," and wiped his hands. She was an old woman and was always afraid.

Told by
Koodloo Pitsualak
aged 75 from
Blacklin Island

Once there was a man with very long hair. He married a young lady who called him different names. One day, the man sang a song, and this is what he sang.

They call me anything;
Maybe I have many names.
They call me anything,
And never say my real name.
Aye, aya, ay, aya.

That is what he sang.

There was a man who wasn't happy to see a ship; he was very scared of them. So they made a song about it. It goes like this.

Aya, Aya, Aya!
Are you scared? Are you scared?
Aya, Aya, Aya, Aya!
Are you scared of people too?
Aya, Aya, Aya, Ya!

Once there were three sisters who went for a walk. As they were walking they were stolen by three ghosts. The people from their camp looked and looked for them but could not find them. The ghosts married the three sisters, but the eldest sister did not forget the way home. She told her sisters never to point the way to their camp. The eldest sister was wise. They escaped without being seen by the ghosts. The ghosts searched for them but could not find them because the sisters hid behind a big rock. So the ghosts gave up and went back home and the sisters returned to their camp.

Long time ago when we were girls, we used to follow boys around. They used to build igloos and we would go inside and play. We collected bones to make *kooliks*. The igloos were very cold. We slept in the igloos even when they were very cold. Our mothers taught us how to work inside them. They did that so we could work when it was cold. Now children are taught in a warm place. It used to be fun when our mothers taught us.

We learned how to play outside, too. We used to go sliding though it was very cold. We never went inside when we were very cold. We had sleds which we made ourselves. We took snow and melted it and put it on our sleds. The melted snow turned to ice and made the sleds go faster.

I remember some stories about things that happened when I was a girl. One was how we went to Nettelling overland by dog team to spend our days until the ice broke. But fall came and we were still there, and we could not get back to our own camp. We were about to starve when my father made a small *kayak* and went hunting. When he came back he had shot two seals. Days went on and again we did not have any food to eat. Our dogs were starving, too. When the dogs died we ate their meat because it was the only food we had. When summer came we had food, but we did not have dogs anymore.

I remember once that three people went hunting from our camp; one

was a white man and one was a woman. A little while later we heard that there were only two people returning and were both very sick. We could hardly recognize the woman because she looked so ill. The white man wanted to stay at our home, and so he did. Then three days later he died. When I heard that he was dead I was very happy. I said, "Good, the white man is dead!" But my parents were afraid when he died. Not long after we moved from the camp.

One time when I was older we went to Blacklin Island to get a boat. We were all women and I was the leader. When we got there, we put the boat on top of the *kamootik* and returned to our camp. On the way back I saw something that looked like a boat. I asked the other women to look at that thing and they, too, said that it was a boat. There were men in it and they were headed toward us. One of the men came to us and said he wanted us to join them. We got on the *kamootik* and started to go to them. We were close when we heard them singing. The reason they were singing was that they had just killed a whale. They had to wait until the tide was out before they could get the whale out of the water and cut up the meat. The women helped the men. They were cutting whale meat for several days. I used to see many whales when I was a teenager. Once I saw an old man shooting at a whale, and he got it, too.

We used to be happy at our camp. Our men used to hunt for about six months down by the edge of the water. We used to be happy at our camp. It's not the same now as when I lived at camp long time ago.

There was a time

Told by
Joanasie Kakee
aged 67
from Sowmeanie

There was a time when there wasn't even one white man. We used to live in a camp called Sowmeanie. An Eskimo took my father to that camp; that's how we started living there. Nobody had been living there before. There were many animals then. I was only a small boy when we lived there. There were two other families with us.

I used to follow my older brother around when he went hunting for caribou. The place where we used to hunt was far away from Sowmeanie. Sometimes it used to take us ten days to reach that place. We only used our sealskin boats to travel in the summertime. As far as I remember, my brother used to have one boat. When I got older we had two boats. I used to be so slow when I was small that when we had to walk my brother used to tie a rope around my waist so I could keep up with him. He used to teach me many things about hunting. When I got to know the things that I was taught how to do, I went to hunt on my own.

One time my brother gave me five dogs, and that was the happiest day of my life. They were my first dogs. I really needed dogs of my own. My dogs grew big and were good dogs. When I hunted with my brothers I was always in the lead because my dogs were very healthy and they were very strong. They had enough meat to eat; I never missed a day of feeding them. I looked after them pretty good. When we came to Pangnirtung to buy the things that we needed and saw the dogs there — they were very dirty — I thought to myself, "The owner should look after his dogs better than this." But then I didn't know what was going to happen to my dogs.

When we moved to Pangnirtung my dogs got dirty and some hairs came off from their skins. It's no good to laugh at other people because sometimes the same can happen to you.

Once I was out hunting when I saw something very black. I thought it was a group of people. But when I got closer I saw that it was a polar bear. I untied two dogs. They surrounded the bear and I killed it. The bear was on thin ice and fell into the water. My dogs had to pull it out. It took us a long time. It was my first catch of a bear.

I told my brother about the bear, and I told him that my dogs were very strong, and he gave me two more dogs. After that I went to further places to hunt. I always preferred to hunt alone because it was more fun. Once I spent thirty-one days hunting before I finally went back to the camp to see how my family was doing. They weren't starving but they were short of food.

When my older brother hunted it seemed to me that he never got tired. I used to get very tired but he wouldn't stop to rest. Also, he wanted to be the only one to shoot the animals. He was bossy then and I hated him for it. It was fun hunting polar bears but he was the only person allowed to shoot them. Sometimes I would listen to him and sometimes I wouldn't.

We both had dog teams. Mine was faster than my brother's; so one day, when we were hunting, I shot a polar bear while my brother was very far from me. When he caught up with me and saw the polar bear I had just shot, he got very angry. He told me not to shoot any more polar bears when he wasn't around. Later, I saw two more polar bears. This time I waited for him and I let him kill them. He was all smiles and good for a while. Boy, he used to be so bossy and greedy. He used to treat me as if I were his servant. He used to treat me like a child that didn't know his own mind. He used to be very mean to us. He wanted everything. He wanted meats, too. He was the only person to get meat, and often we had to buy the things we needed. But, then, he was the boss. But he never thought of others. He wasn't rich either. I hope he realizes the terrible things he did to us. He was always like that before we came to Pangnirtung. Now he's a different person.

I remember one day I heard someone call my name and I looked around, but I couldn't see anybody. As it turned out, it was my brother calling me to help him. He had fallen into the water. As I went down to help him I saw polar bears. I didn't bother to help him; instead, I ran to get my rifle. When my brother saw what I was doing, he sprang out of the water and ran after the polar bears! I killed one and two other persons got two more. My brother didn't get any. But he wanted to get the polar bear skin. So I gave it to him. I was feeling cheated. When we headed home I started to dislike him even more than ever. Me and my younger brother used to talk about our stupid brother, and we decided never to go out with him again. We didn't, and he seemed to change a bit after that.

When my father was too old to hunt he instructed us on what to do when we went out. He told me always to carry my rifle on my back in case

I saw a polar bear or any other animal. Some polar bears can hide pretty well. You won't know one's there till it attacks. My father used to tell us many things when he couldn't hunt anymore. In those days we used to have plenty of animals, but now in Pangnirtung there are not too many. That was when there weren't any white people and when we lived in our old way of life. I sure miss it.

In Sowmeanie there were lots of animals, and we had enough meat to feed our family. In 1952, we were told to move to Pangnirtung. They said that we had to stay in one place; so everybody went to Pangnirtung. Some people were picked up by an airplane. My family left on the plane one time when I was away hunting. When I came back and heard that my family had gone on the plane to Pangnirtung I got angry and started to shoot my dogs. After that I went to Pangnirtung. I told my relatives that I shot all the dogs because I didn't want to leave my home. There were so many animals in Sowmeanie. I didn't want to leave the animals that we hunted every day. I was very unhappy to leave my home. When I think of Sowmeanie, I want to live there again, but it's too far from Pangnirtung.

Even when I got sick, I didn't stop working because we needed food, and my family depended on me to get some meat. Sometimes, if I got sick when I was hunting I would lie down for awhile, and if I was too sick to continue to hunt I would go back to the camp. After I came to Pangnirtung I was told to go to the hospital; they told me that I was to leave right away to some hospital in the south. That was in 1958.

In springtime, I once went caribou hunting with my sister, and I had many dogs with me. When we got to the place, we began to look for caribou. We found one, and I gave a shot but it didn't die because I did not have good bullets. I had to hammer my bullets before I started to shoot; if I didn't hammer them they wouldn't work. My rifle was in very bad condition; it was old. We looked for more caribou and finally we found a herd of them. I killed one, and we rushed home so our family could have some meat to eat. When we got there, my brother wasn't back from hunting. So the next day I started to search for him. I thought he must have died out there. When I found him he was in a land alone. I brought him with me when I started heading for home.

We were free to live anywhere in the land before the white people showed up. After that we couldn't live freely like we used to. Everything was free and we did not have any rules. We can't go to our past even if we want to. I think it's better to live like we used to. I miss our old way of life.

I used to be a very brave man, now that I think of it. I used to be crazy sometimes, too!